Christmas, 1976

To Daddy,

with love from

Diane, Walker

& Greg

A *terra magica* BOOK

HANNS REICH

Horses

HILL AND WANG · NEW YORK
A division of Farrar, Straus and Giroux, Inc.

Hast thou given the horse strength? Hast thou clothed his neck with thunder? Canst thou make him afraid as a grasshopper? The glory of his nostrils is terrible. He paweth in the valley, and rejoiceth in his strength: he goeth on to meet the armed men. He mocketh at fear, and is not affrighted; neither turneth he back from the sword. The quiver rattleth against him, the glittering spear and the shield. He swalloweth the ground with fierceness and rage: neither believeth he that it is the sound of the trumpet. He saith among the trumpets, Ha, ha! and he smelleth the battle afar off, the thunder of the captains and the shouting.

Book of Job

The Chariot Race at Patroclus' Funeral Games from Homer's Iliad

Meantime the Grecians in a ring beheld
The coursers bounding o'er the dusty field.
The first who mark'd them was the Cretan king;
High on a rising ground, above the ring,
The monarch sat; from whence with sure survey
He well observed the chief who led the way,
And heard from far his animating cries,
And saw the foremost steed with sharpen'd eyes;
On whose broad front a blaze of shining white,
Like the full moon stood obvious to the sight.
He saw; and, rising, to the Greeks begun:
"Are yonder horse discern'd by me alone?
Or can ye, all, another chief survey,
And other steeds, than lately led the way?"

No sooner had he spoke, but thundering near,
Drives, through a stream of dust, the charioteer;
High o'er his head the circling lash he wields;
His bounding horses scarcely touch the fields:
His car amidst the dusty whirlwind roll'd,
Bright with the mingled blaze of tin and gold,
Refulgent through the cloud: no eye could find
The track his flying wheels had left behind:
And the fierce coursers urged their rapid pace
So swift, it seem'd a flight, and not a race.
Now victor at the goal Tydides stands,
Quits his bright car, and springs upon the sands;
From the hot steeds the sweaty torrents stream;
The well-plied whip is hung athwart the beam:

With joy brave Sthenelus receives the prize,
The tripod vase, and dame with radiant eyes:
These to the ships his train triumphant leads
The chief himself unyokes the panting steeds.

Alexander Pope

From King Henry V, Act III, Scene VII

DAUPHIN. I will not change my horse with any that treads on four posterns. Ca ha! he bounds from the earth as if his entrails were hairs; le cheval volant, the Pegasus, chez les narines de feu! When I bestride him, I soar, I am a hawk: he trots the air; the earth sings when he touches it; the basest horn of his hoof is more musical than the pipe of Hermes.

ORLEANS. He's of the colour of the nutmeg.

DAUPHIN. And of the heat of the ginger. It is a beast for Perseus; he is pure air and fire; and the dull elements of earth and water never appear in him, but only in patient stillness while his rider mounts him: he is indeed a horse and all other jades you may call beasts.

CONSTABLE. Indeed, my lord, it is a most absolute and excellent horse.

DAUPHIN. It is the prince of palfreys; his neigh is like the bidding of a monarch, and his countenance enforces homage.

ORLEANS. No more, cousin.

DAUPHIN. Nay, the man hath no wit that cannot, from the rising of the lark to the lodging of the lamb, vary deserved praise on my palfrey: it is a theme as fluent as the sea: turn the sands into eloquent tongues, and my horse is argument for them all.

William Shakespeare

The Common Cart Horse

His form is heavy, his motions slow, and his aspect without sprightliness: He is nevertheless extremely useful, and is employed in the business of agriculture and other domestic concerns.

Till of late years, Pack-Horses were employed, in the northern counties of England, to carry the different manufactures and articles of traffic from one part of the kingdom to another; but the improved state of our roads has caused that mode of conveyance to be almost entirely laid aside. In their journeys over trackless moors, they strictly adhere to the line of order regularity and custom has taught them to observe: The leading Horse, which is always chosen for his sagacity and steadiness, being furnished with bells, gives notice to the rest, who follow the sound, and generally without much deviation, though sometimes at a considerable distance. The following instance will show with what obstinate perseverance they have been known to observe the lines of their order: — Some years ago, one of these Horses, which had been long accustomed to follow his leader, by accident or fatigue, was thrown into an inferior rank: The poor animal, as if sensible of his disgrace, by the most strenuous exertions, at length recovered his usual station, which he maintained during the remainder of the journey; but on his arrival in the inn-yard, he dropped down dead upon the spot, his life falling a sacrifice to his ambition — species of heroism we must admire even in the brute creation.

Thomas Bewick (1790)
History of Quadrupeds

The Blood Horse

Gamarra is a dainty steed,
Strong, black, and of a noble breed,
Full of fire, and full of bone,
With all his line of fathers known;
Fine his nose, his nostrils thin,
But blown abroad by the pride within!
His mane is like a river flowing
And his eyes like embers glowing
In the darkness of the night,
And his pace as swift as light.

Look, how 'round his straining throat
Grace and shifting beauty float!
Sinewy strength is in his reins,
And the red blood gallops through his veins;
Richer, redder, never ran
Through the boasting heart of man.
He can trace his lineage higher
Than the Bourbon dare aspire, —
Douglas, Guzman, or the Guelph,
Or O'Brien's blood itself!

He, who hath no peer, was born,
Here, upon a red March morn;
But his famous fathers dead
Were Arabs all, and Arab bred,
And the last of that great line
Trod like one of a race divine!

And yet, — he was but friend to one
Who fed him at the set of sun,
By some lone fountain fringed with green:
With him, a roving Bedouin,
He lived (none else would he obey
Through all the hot Arabian day),
And died untamed upon the sands
Where Balkh amidst the desert stands.

Bryan Waller Procter (1787–1874)

Captions

Cover: *Anita Schmidt*

1. Stone Age drawing in the Niaux Cave (Arège, France). *André Held – R. Laffont*
2. Evening on a farm. *Hans W. Silvester*
3. Horse galloping — a photographic impression. *Anita Schmidt*
4. The small white horses of Camargue, an alluvial island in the Rhone delta. *Hans W. Silvester*
6. Many of the exercises developed in the past for the use of cavalry in time of war have become obsolete, yet Johann Elias Ridinger's famous engravings, which were made around 1760, still decorate the walls of harness rooms and the apartments of horse lovers all the world over. *Meisenbach*
7. *Anita Schmidt – Anthony*
8. Iceland ponies have been bred for more than a thousand years. For three-quarters of the year they are left to their own resources and live in a completely wild state. In the spring the herds leave the coastal regions and wander slowly toward the hills of the interior in search of pasture. On their day-long wanderings, they cross countless ice-cold streams. Struggling with the whirlpools makes the ponies courageous and strong. *Thorsteinn Jósepsson*
9. A Tyrolean pony called the Haflinger (see pictures 34 and 35) walking along a glacier. *Hein Gorny*
10. Rider with lasso on Camargue Island (see picture 4). *Francisco Hidalgo*
11. Rounding up horses near Mount Kenya in Africa. *Ulrich Mack*
13. A herd of horses in Africa. *Ulrich Mack*
14. Riding in the Pacific Ocean near Hollywood. *Hanns Hubmann*
15. Mont-Saint-Michel at low tide. *Heidemaria Weiss*
16. Ancient Greek vase painting (Antiquarium, Berlin). *Foto Marburg*
17. Young stallions playfully fighting. *Gunnar Cornelius – Bavaria*
18. One of the sculptured horses flanking the avenue leading to the tombs of the Chinese Emperors of the Ming Dynasty (Peking, China). *Paolo Koch*
19. Iceland ponies spend the winter on the coast. A warm woolly coat up to ten centimeters thick protects them against the cold. They push at the snow with their noses to find food, or if the snow is frozen they plough it up with their hooves. Like all wild animals, Iceland ponies are well adapted to their natural environment and can survive hardship without human help. *Thorsteinn Jósepsson*
20. Shetland pony. *Edith Rimkus*
22. A ten-year-old Hanover. *Gerhard Hanig – Anthony*
23. *Comet*
24. *Walter Luden – Ernst Leitz*
25. Returning home to the stud farm at sunset. This is one of the old photographs which has become a classic in horse photography. *Hein Gorny*
26. Mare with foal on Camargue Island (see picture 4). *Hans W. Silvester*
27. A gypsy pilgrimage on Camargue Island is not complete without the accompanying Guardians on horseback. *Ernst Grasser – Bavaria*
28. "Tally-ho!" *George Konig – Hecht*
29. Huntsmen in the Chantilly woods (France). *Hans W. Silvester*
30. In the Mehrfeld Marshes near Dülmen (Westphalia). In this region of forests, meadows, and marshland, about 200 horses live wild. Once a year the herds are rounded up in compounds and the year-old stallions are branded with the mark of the Herzog von Croy. *Peter Thomann*
31. Two foals. *Peter Thomas – Bavaria*

65. A holy horse at the Temple of Ise in Japan. Horses are dedicated to one of the Goddesses, rich Japanese giving live horses, and the poorer ones clay horses. *Paul Almasy*
66. Blacksmith's shop in Spain. *Josip Ciganovic – laenderpress*
67. *Henry Cartier Bresson – Magnum*
68. *Peter Thomas – Bavaria*
69. Pony with foal. *Erhard Jorde*
70. In Hungary five horses are harnessed to a carriage instead of the usual two or four. *Hein Gorny*
71. The famous purebred Trakehner stallion Famulus. *Werner Menzendorf*
72. Fritz Thiedemann on Meteor making their last public appearance in July 1961. Thiedemann won 550 prizes in his career and Meteor 150. *Fritz Peyer*

Croupade à
gauche.

Crouppade
links.

Croupada ad
sinistram.

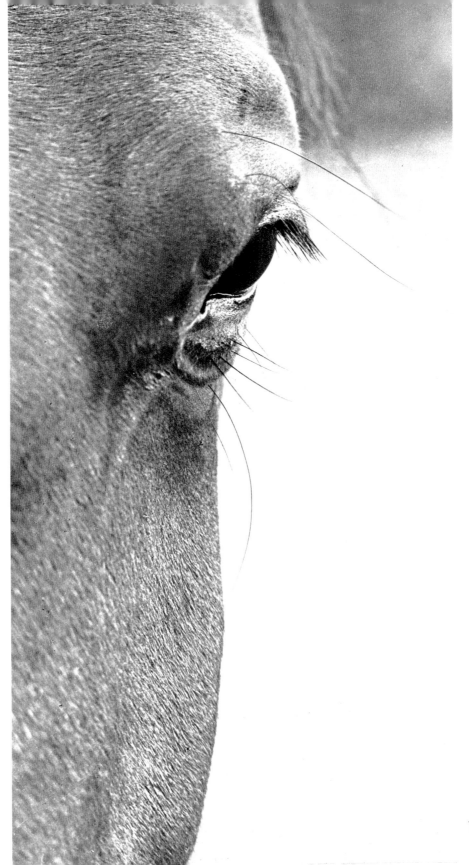

13

16

22

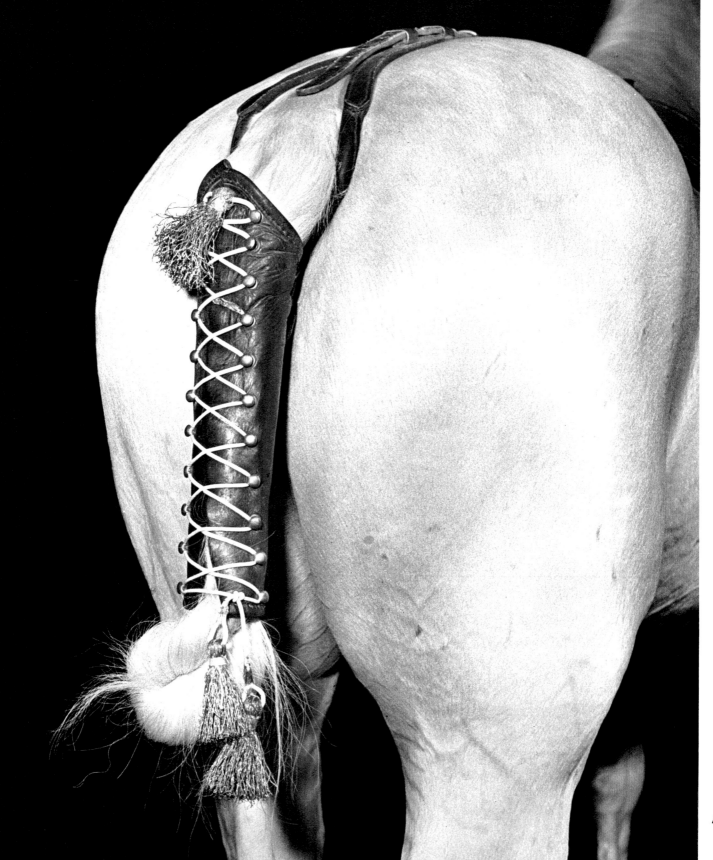